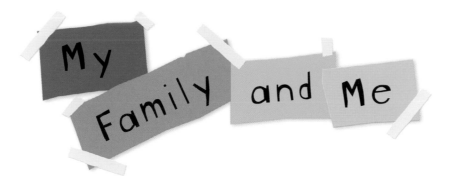

Celebrating a Birthday

Mary Auld

SEA-TO-SEA
Mankato Collingwood London

Everyone has a birthday every year. It's the day we were born. Ellie is six today.

? Your turn...
When is your birthday?
How old will you be?

4

We give people presents on their birthday. Pete's mom and dad gave him a bicycle. His brother, Adam, helped them choose it.

66 Adam says...

"I went with Mom to the store. I knew Pete would like a yellow bike."

Joe gave his brother a fun game on his birthday.

Annie and Patrick gave their grandma some bubble bath.

? Your turn...
Why do you think families give each other presents?

It's nice to give birthday cards, too. Mingyu made a card for her mom.

Lotte drew a boat for her dad.

Lotte says...
"Dad always says he wants a boat."

Birthdays are days for special treats. Lee's mom took him and his friends to the zoo.

Lois spent her birthday
in the park.

? Your turn...

What special treat would you
like on your birthday?

Annie and Karl took their mom breakfast in bed on her birthday.

66 Karl says...
"Mom ate it all up—
even the burned toast!"

Lots of people have birthday parties. Hayley's aunt came before her party to help with the cooking.

? Your turn...

Have you had a birthday party?
Who helped to get it ready?
What kind of food did you have?

Jagdish had fun at his birthday party. His friends and family came. There was a clown.

> 66 Jagdish says...
>
> "We all laughed a lot."

On Nia's first birthday, all the family helped blow out the candle on her cake.

Paul blew out all the candles by himself.

? Your turn...

What do people sing when they light the candles on a birthday cake?

Some birthdays are more important than others. The whole family got together for Adam's grandpa's 70th birthday.

Adam says...

"Everyone was there—my mom, dad, sister, and grandma, and all my uncles, aunts, and cousins. Grandpa looked really happy."

How do you and your family celebrate your birthday?

Some Things to Do

When is your birthday? When are your family and friends' birthdays? Find out all the dates and make a birthday book.

Pretend it is someone in your family's birthday and plan a surprise party for them. Make lists of who you will invite, what food you will eat, and what games you will play.

Design a birthday card for someone in your family, with a picture of something he or she likes.

Write a poem or tell a story about the best birthday present ever.

About this book

The aim of this book is to give children the opportunity to explore what their family means to them and their role within it in a positive and celebratory way. In particular it emphasizes the importance of care and support within the family. It also encourages children to compare their own experiences with other people, recognizing similarities and differences and respecting these as part of daily life.

Children will get pleasure out of looking at this book on their own. However, sharing the book on a one-to-one basis or within a group will also be very rewarding. Just talking about the main text and pictures is a good starting point, and the panels also prompt discussion:
• Question panels ask children to talk directly about their own experiences and feelings.
• Quote panels encourage them to think further by comparing their experiences with those of other children.

This edition first published in 2011 by
Sea-to-Sea Publications
Distributed by Black Rabbit Books
P.O. Box 3263, Mankato, Minnesota 56002

Printed in China, Dongguan

Library of Congress Cataloging-in-Publication Data

Auld, Mary.
  Celebrating a birthday / Mary Auld.
    p. cm. -- (My family and me)
  ISBN 978-1-59771-229-3 (library binding)
  1. Birthdays--Juvenile literature. I. Title.
  GT2430.A85 2011
  394.2--dc22
                                          2009051541

9 8 7 6 5 4 3 2

Published by arrangement with the Watts Publishing Group Ltd, London.

Series editor: Rachel Cooke
Art director: Jonathan Hair
Design: Jason Anscomb

Picture credits: Meiko Arquillos/zefa/Corbis: 9. John-Francis Bourke/zefa/Corbis: 14. Gareth Brown/Corbis: 8. Owen Franken/Corbis: 18. Grace/zefa/Corbis: 3 Sally Greenhill/Sally & Richard Greenhill: 10, 21. Richard Hutchings/Corbis: Cover, 22. Richard T. Nowitz/Corbis: 6. Ulrike Preuss/Photofusion: 11, 17. Paula Solloway /Photofusion: 19. LWA-Dann Tardif/Corbis: 13. Bob Watkins/Photofusion: 7. Stephanie Weiler/zefa/Corbis: 4. Every attempt has been made to clear copyright. Should there be any inadvertent omission please apply to the publisher for rectification.

Please note that some of the pictures in this book have been posed by models.

March 2010
RD/6000006414/002